DOLLAR STORE CRAFTS & RECIPES

Volume One

By Victor Rook

A Rook Communications Publication

Publisher:
Rook Communications
P.O. Box 571
Manassas, VA 20108

Email: vic@victorrook.com

Website: victorrook.com

ISBN-10: 0-9766653-6-0
ISBN-13: 978-0-9766653-6-6

Cover and interior design by Victor Rook

TABLE OF CONTENTS

WHERE TO FIND ITEMS:

Though this book is not affiliated with any particular dollar store, all the crafts and recipes within this volume were made from items purchased at Dollar Tree. For convenience, I've placed images of each item in its original packaging on the materials pages so it will be easier for you to locate them. Some items may be seasonal. Happy crafting!

CRAFT 1: JURASSIC HERB TERRARIUM

Create this terrific dinosaur world and watch it grow! Children will enjoy making it, and parents can use the herbs for recipes. Fun for the kids, food for the family!

Materials:
Plastic planter, clear punch bowl
Dry moss, rocks, potting soil
Dinosaurs or plastic creatures
Herb kits/seeds (sold in spring)

Tools:
Water mister

Estimated Time: 30 minutes

Level: Easy

Cost: About $7 with leftover soil and rocks.

Step 1:
Fill container with an inch of small rocks, then cover with a layer of sphagnum moss. This will allow water to drain through.

Step 2:
Add soil to about two inches from the top.

Step 3:
Arrange rocks and dinosaurs. Here I have sectioned off different places for the herbs to grow and made a dinosaur ring in the center.

Step 4:
Add 2-3 cups of water evenly to moisten soil. Spread seed packets to cover areas. Press into soil or cover with a fine layer of dirt.

Step 5:
Mist the top thoroughly. Water when needed.

Step 6:
Cover with the dome and place in bright, indirect light (not full sun). Watch it grow!

CRAFT 2: MAGIC MARKER MUGS

Create decorative mugs with your own designs! Why pay five or more dollars when you can make one the way you want for little over a dollar? Great candy and pencil holders.

Materials:
White ceramic mugs
Permanent markers

Tools:
Rubbing alcohol

Estimated Time: 1 hour

Level: Easy

Cost: About $1 per mug! Markers can be used many times.

Cheap ceramic mugs with a thin glaze work the best. This one was purchased at Dollar Tree.

These were the marker brands purchased at Dollar Tree for this craft. Other markers may or may not work better or at all.

Step 1:

Remove tag from mug so it does not burn in the oven.

Step 2:

Clean the mug with soap and water or rubbing alcohol. Allow to thoroughly dry.

Step 3:

Apply your design with the permanent markers. Avoid touching the surface by holding the cup with your hand inside or press down on top with the bottom of the mug on a flat surface. Keep your designs below where lips would drink, about 1/2".

Tip: If you make a mistake, remove mistake thoroughly with rubbing alcohol on a cloth. Allow to dry before reapplying design.

Step 3:

Allow your design to dry for 48 hours.

Step 4:

Place your mug(s) on a metal pan and into the oven. Then turn the oven to 375° F and wait 20 minutes. **Do not preheat the oven**; you want the mugs to warm and cool with the oven. After 20 minutes, turn the oven off and **keep the mugs inside for at least two hours to cool with the oven**. DO NOT open the oven door until then.

Note: Though the oven baking helps cure the design, it is still best to hand wash the mugs with a gentle sponge instead of dishwashing, which may remove the design over time.

I like to use the mugs to hold my markers and pens. Fill them with candy and give them away as gifts!

CRAFT 3: BUTTERFLY POT HANGER

Make a weather-resistant pot hanger from one bundle of cord. This beautiful mustard-colored Poly Rope was purchased at Dollar Tree. Hang your plants outdoors or inside.

Materials:
(1) 50-foot polypropylene cord

Tools:
Scissors, Ruler

Estimated Time:
Approx. 1 hour

Level: Intermediate

Cost: Just $1!

This cord also comes in brown at Dollar Tree.

Step 1:
Cut six 100" (8'4") cords. This will use up the entire 50-foot bundle. Make sure you pull the cords tight when you measure.

Step 2:
Bring the ends of the cords together and fold in half. Make sure they are even and you find the dead center. Then tie an overhand knot about 3" from the top to form a hanging loop.

Step 3:
Pull individual cords to tighten the knot. Loosen if you have to adjust cords.

Step 4:
Hang the top loop on something sturdy. Here I used an S hook. You'll want to be able to pull down to keep knots tight and even.

Step 5:
Separate the cords into three groups of four. Try to choose cords that are close together so it looks nice up top.

Step 6:

About a foot down from the top of the hanger loop, tie the first half of a square knot using one set of four cords. Keeping the two center cords taut, place the left cord over the center cords and under the right cord, then the right cord under the center cords and over the left.

Step 7:

Repeat the above, but go under the center cords with the left cord and over with the right cord like the image below.

Step 8:

Tighten the knot while pulling all cords taut.

Step 9:

Tie another square knot about 2" below.

Step 10:

Push the bottom knot up to form loops.

Step 11:

Repeat steps 9 & 10 about 1" down to make two smaller loops. A butterfly!

Step 12:
Repeat the butterfly knot on the other two sets of four cords. I offset the other knots a few inches. Just make sure the lowest knot is no more than 14" down from the top of the hanger loop.

Step 13:
Using four cords from adjacent butterfly knots (two from each), tie a square knot about 18" down from the top of the hanger. Keep cords taut. Tie two more with the other adjacent cords. These are called alternating square knots and form the pot sling. Make sure you pick the correct cords.

Step 14:
Tie another row of alternating square knots about 4" below the first.

Step 15:
Tie an overhand knot about 2-1/2" below the last row of square knots. Pull cords tight.

Step 16:
Trim and fray the remaining ends. You should have barely any cord left.

CRAFT 4: PAPER BAG FLOWERS & TREES

Make decorative rustic flowers from simple paper bags. This craft also includes paper bag trees that children can make at the same time. Something for everyone!

Materials:
4 Paper bags/flower, 1 per tree
Poster board (for petal template)

Tools:
Scissors, Glue stick
Tape, String (to hang flower)

Estimated Time:
Flower: 30 min. Tree: 5 min.

Level: Tree-Easy
Flower-Intermediate

Cost: 10 flowers for $1.25!

Step 1:
With the bottom flap in front, cut along the top edge of the flap. Keep the bottoms to create little goodie bags for later!

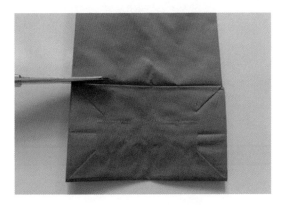

Step 2:
Cut off the section of the bag with the curved indent. You can discard that piece.

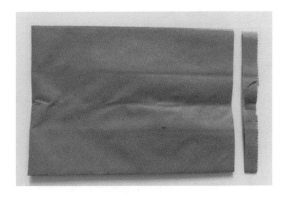

Step 3:
Trace the edge of the bag onto a piece of poster board, then cut it out.

Step 4:
Draw a petal shape on the poster board with a pointed tip and a flat bottom. Make it almost as wide as the poster board.

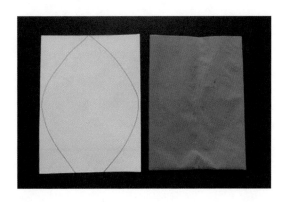

Step 5:
Cut out the petal template.

Step 6:
Hold the template onto each bag so the tip touches the top, and carefully cut along the edges. Repeat steps 1, 2, and 6 on four bags. Keep the scrap pieces for later.

Step 7:
You will end up with two large petals and two small petals per bag. How cool is that!

Step 8:
Fold the large petals in half and crease.

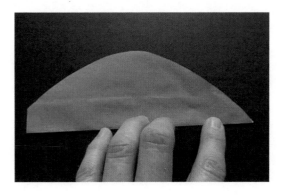

Step 9:
Apply glue stick to the base of each petal and glue them together into a rosette one at a time. Glue, add petal, glue, add petal, etc. Keep the leaves from flattening too much.

Step 10:
Do the same with the smaller petals until you have two rosettes.

Step 11:
Glue the smaller rosette onto the center of the larger rosette. Offset the leaves a bit.

Step 12:
Scrunch up a piece of scrap bag and glue it to the center of the flower. Tape a small loop of string to the back just above center to hang.

Step 1:
With the bag flat, cut several lines from the top to the middle. You can offset them a bit to make lower or higher branches.

Step 3:
Twist two nearby flaps of paper together at a time to form branches, or curl each separate flap with a pencil for a curly tree!

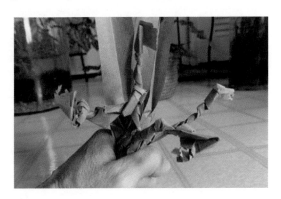

Step 2:
Open up the bag, then grab it by the middle and twist tightly several times. This will form the trunk. Press the bottom onto a hard surface at the same time to form a flat base.

Step 4:
Bend the branches into place to create the finished tree. Use a large bag for a big tree!

CRAFT 5: BUTTERFLY JAR

Add a bit of nature anywhere with this gorgeous butterfly jar. Search out the craft sections for different butterflies—or use birds! Make sure they have wires attached.

Materials:
Glass vase with wide middle
Butterfly with wire attached
Bag of moss balls

Tools:
Scissors

Estimated Time: 5 minutes

Level: Easy

Cost: $3 with leftover butterfly.

Step 1:
Place all but one moss ball into the vase. Arrange so that the last moss ball can be placed level on top.

Step 2:
Cut wire on underside of butterfly to about 1-1/4". Bend at a 90-degree angle.

Note: Don't let the kids poke themselves!

Step 3:
Poke butterfly into last moss ball by holding the body. Be careful not to harm the wings.

Step 4:
Place moss ball with butterfly attached into the vase so that the wings can spread wide open. You may need to adjust the other moss balls to get it to fit properly. Use a pencil or a thin stick to move them around.

Note: Things tend to fade in bright sunlight, so keep indoors away from the window. It looks great in a bathroom or on a bookshelf!

CRAFT 6: COLORED PUSH CANDLES

Add an instant glow to any room with portable colored push candles. Great for parties, or use several to create a relaxing ambiance in the bathroom or bedroom.

Materials:
Bag of colored glass gems
Glass holder about 3" diameter
Black LED push light
3 AAA batteries

Tools:
Scissors to remove items

Estimated Time: 5 minutes

Level: Easy

Cost: $4 with leftover battery.

Step 1:
Place a single layer of gems on the bottom of the glass holder to level out the push light if it does not rest flat on the bottom.

Step 2:
Place the batteries into the push light and set it level on top of the gems.

Tip: Though the black push light won't really be visible in the dark, you may want to conceal it with a ribbon around the outside. Or use a wide container so gems hide sides.

Step 3:
Pour just enough gems on top of the push light to almost the top of the glass holder.

Step 4:
Turn the light on and off by pushing your finger through the gems and onto the light.

CRAFT 7: WRITERS GIFT BOX

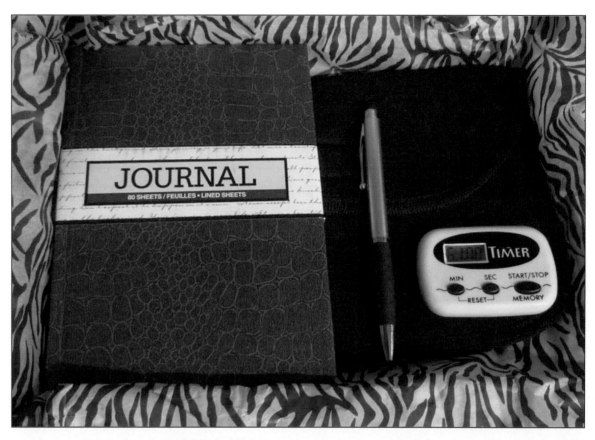

Create theme boxes for hobbies and interests. This box is designed for aspiring writers and includes a journal, a stylus pen, an egg timer (to portion writing time) and a tablet sleeve to hold everything. An actual 7" tablet can be swapped with the paper journal, too.

Materials:
Journal, Tablet Sleeve
Egg Timer, Stylus Pen
Gift box (3-pack)
Tissue Paper (8-pack)

Tools:
Tape for inside box corners

Estimated Time: 10 minutes

Level: Easy

Cost: Under $5 with single gift box and one tissue wrap.

Inside of Box:

Fold a single piece of tissue paper into the taped box, then arrange your contents.

Or insert the journal and pen into the sleeve and attach the timer with a thin ribbon.

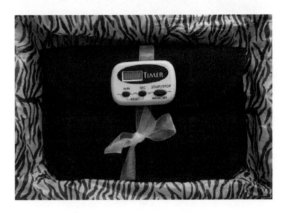

Multiple Uses:

The sleeves are meant to hold tablets, too!

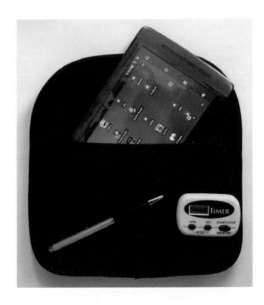

Outside of Box:

Spruce up the box with a customized label. Here I wrote the word "WRITE" on a chalk label and applied it to the lid.

Tip: To make the chalk not wipe off, apply a wide piece of clear shipping tape over the label before removing it, then cut it out inside the peel line. Remove backing and apply to box.

You can also print your own labels.

CRAFT 8: BEAD STORAGE CASE

Create a portable bead storage kit for your crafting and jewelry needs. This hardware storage case from Dollar Tree comes complete with a place to store a pair of tweezers, thread, and wire, as well as a ruler on top in centimeters. Find it in the tool aisle.

Materials:
Tool Bench® Storage Case
Tweezers
Assorted bead packets

Tools:
Scissors, rubbing alcohol

Estimated Time: 15 minutes

Level: Easy

Cost: $4 as shown including two assorted bead packets.

Step 1:
Choose a plastic storage case where the lid is flat to the top (not buckled or warped) so small beads won't shuffle into other compartments. Carefully remove the label.

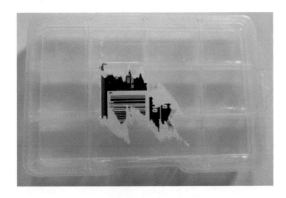

Step 2:
Use rubbing alcohol to remove remaining label and sticky residue.

Step 3:
Carefully open the bead packets. Cut through the tape on the bottom. They don't make these things easy to open without spilling.

Step 4:
I used the cardboard packaging for the tweezers to cover various bead compartments while transferring them to the plastic case.

Step 5:
Use the tweezers to pick up beads while working on your projects.

Tip: You'll notice that this particular plastic case from Dollar Tree has a ruler on top measuring up to 10 centimeters. This may come in handy when measuring wire or thread.

CRAFT 9: FRIENDSHIP BRACELETS

Friendship bracelets go back many years, but have gained a resurgence recently. Learn in this craft how to make friendship bracelets in a simple braid and two chevron patterns. You can also make quick and easy bracelets from headwraps and ponytail holders.

Materials:
String or embroidery floss
Headwraps for instant bracelets

Tools:
Scissors, Ruler, Clipboard

Estimated Time: 10 minutes to 4 hours depending on design.

Level: Easy to Intermediate

Cost: Approx. $.50 for string bracelet. Six instant bracelets for just $1.00.

Step 1:
Cut four cords of different colors at least 2 yards (72") long. Fold in half.

Step 2:
Tie the cords together with an overhand knot about 3/4" down from the fold.

Step 3:
Flip the knot over and place under a clipboard clamp to hold your work in place. Separate the cords into two groups of four so the colors are a mirror version of each other on the left and right-hand sides. This is important. In this bracelet I used two cords of blue, one cord of light purple (mauve) and one cord of pink. Eight cords when folded.

Step 4:
Working only on the left-hand side, grab the outermost cord and cross it over the other three. This cord is known as the leader cord. The other cords will knot around this.

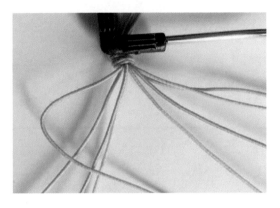

Step 5:
Take the first cord (purple), and loop around the leader cord (blue) as shown. This is the first half of a double half-hitch knot. While keeping the leader cord taut, pull the knot up.

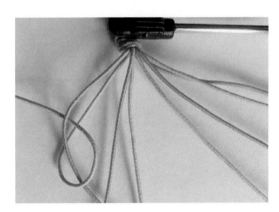

Step 6:
Tie another knot exactly the same as the first.

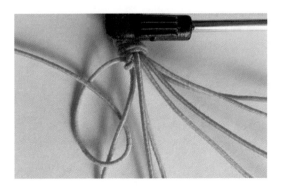

Step 7:
Repeat the double half-hitch knot for the next two cords on the left side. Keeping the leader cord taut across the working cords while you pull up the knots makes them fall into place better. The first row may look a little funky.

Step 8:
Move the four left-hand cords to the side and work on the right-hand side. Cross the right outermost cord over the other three like so.

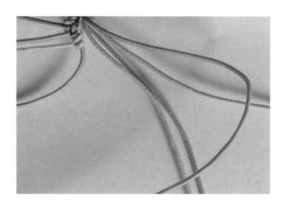

Step 9:
Create a half-hitch knot in the opposite direction like so. Then make another one.

Step 10:
Form double half-hitch knots with the other two cords on the right-hand side. Then, create one more double half-hitch knot with the left-hand side leader (the inner blue cord now) under the right-hand leader. In other words, use the left-hand-side inner cord as if it were a fourth cord on the right-hand side. This final knot will swap the leaders from left to right sides and form the vertex knot.

Step 11:
Start back on the left-hand side again and repeat another row. Then right-hand side, then the vertex knot. Make sure you use the correct cords. It becomes easier once a row or two is tied. You'll see your V-shaped chevron pattern start to form.

Step 12:
Check now and then to see how the bracelet fits around your wrist. Stop knotting when the top of the loop meets the bottom row.

Step 13:
Now it's time to create tails at the bottom. Braid the left cords about 2" long and tie a knot at the end, then braid the right cords together. Because it's much easier to braid with three cords than four when using small cord, I chose to combine two of the cords here (a blue and purple) as if they were one.

Once you've finished both braids and knotted the ends, cut the excess cord. Leave 1/8".

How to Braid:
If you've never braided before, you simply cross the left-hand cord over the center cord, then cross the right-hand cord over that cord (now the new center). Left over center, right over center, left over center, right over center, etc. Work your fingers close to the end of the braid so the braid isn't too loose.

TYING YOUR BRACELET:

With a Friend:
Place the bracelet around your wrist and insert one of the tails into the loop. Knot that tail with the other tail so it fits comfortably. Let the tails hang down, flatten to your wrist, or you can twist them around the bracelet.

Adjustable knot and fitting on yourself:
Before putting the bracelet on, take the two tails and pull them through the loop. Keep pulling the rest of the bracelet through until you are almost back to the loop.

Insert the tails into the new loop formed.

Now pull the original loop the rest of the way so it forms a Lark's Head knot over the tails.

Lightly tighten the knot and pull it to the end of the tails. It should stop at the tail knots.

Pull the bracelet onto your wrist. You may have to manipulate and squeeze your hand to fit it on. Then pull the tails to tighten and adjust the bracelet. Voila!

To remove the bracelet, pull the wide end of the bracelet before the tails to make it bigger.

Other Patterns:

There are many patterns for friendship bracelets. Create this chevron pattern by using 8 cords of two colors (4 cords in half). Begin with one color on the left and the other on the right before knotting.

Tip: Most dollar stores don't have a wide selection of cord colors. You can try white cotton string or jute if you want. I made this bracelet with an inexpensive brown cord packet from Walmart.

INSTANT FRIENDSHIP BRACELETS:

If you're looking for quick and easy bracelets with what's available at Dollar Tree, look no further than these elastic headwraps.

They come in mixed shades of brown, blue, black, and white. Just loop one or two twice over your wrist and you're good to go.

If two loops are too loose, you can make this quick knot in the center to take up slack. In this diagram it appears I am going to tie a knot by bringing Loop 1 over and around Loop 2 and up through the center (2). Instead, you want Loop 1 to come up through the spot marked 1. Once you've done that, pull Loop 1 and Loop 2 to form a knot.

One of the cords in the knot will allow you to slide the loops to make them even.

For Children:
Many dollar stores carry elastic ponytail holders that the kids can share as bracelets. Just make sure they're not on too tight and you might want to stretch them beforehand.

CRAFT 10: NATURAL BIRD'S NEST

Make this lovely bird's nest from a roll of sisal twine. Hang it as an ornament or place a group in a decorative basket. The fraying twine gives it a natural look.

Materials:
Sisal Twine (180-foot roll)
Smallest decorative bird

Tools:
Scissors, Ruler
White glue
Pencil or crochet hook

Estimated Time: 4-5 hours

Level: Advanced

Cost: $1.50 with leftover bird.

Step 1:
Cut 38 cords at 1-1/2 yards (54") each, and one cord 2-1/2 yards (90") long.

Step 2:
Line up the ends of all 39 cords and tie an overhand knot about an inch from the top. Pull the knot tight.

Step 3:
With the knot upside down in your hand, spread the cords out as evenly as possible. You may want to place the knot in between your knees or in a vice for ease of work.

Note: Take time to evenly spread out the cords. Otherwise, you may run into problems with cords not falling directly in place, which may cause a lopsided sphere.

Pull the 2-1/2 yard cord up and cross over the top of the other cords in a spiral. This is your leader cord that other cords will loop around in the following steps.

Step 4:
Tie double half-hitch knots (Page 23, Steps 5 and 6) around the leader cord in a spiral. You will want to only use about six of the 38 cords to make the initial spiral small and tight. Pick ones that are evenly spaced (about every 6th cord). This is a little tricky at first, so be patient.

Step 5:
Continue to tie double half-hitch knots for a second row with about every fourth cord. You are skipping cords because the spiral is small. As you continue to the third and fourth rows and so on, you'll use more cords. It's okay to tie a single half-hitch knot with some cords just to start to incorporate them. Use your best judgment.

Tip: Sisal twine likes to fray and splinter all over and bits of it will fall to the floor, so I suggest working on the knots outdoors.

Step 6:
As you get out to about the fourth spiral, start pushing the shape into a sphere top.

Step 7:
Once you are sure all cords have been used, turn the shape over, untie the large knot, and cut the ends to about half an inch. This will prevent the knot from getting in the way as you continue the spiral.

Step 8:
Turn back over and continue with more rows.

Step 9:
After the sixth spiral (or when it looks like the top middle of sphere), turn the leader back and go in the opposite direction. Go almost all the way around, but leave six cords free for the opening (don't use them).

Step 10:
Reverse the leader cord and repeat Step 9 until you have added four rows.

Step 11:
Now do another row using all cords. The six unused cords will look like a jail cell.

Step 12:
Continue to tie more knots while gradually using fewer cords so the bottom spirals are smaller. It may be easier to flip the shape over to work on it. Make the last spiral as tight as you can. It will not be as small as the top spiral because of the cords in the middle.

Step 13:
Cut the cords off to about half an inch.

Step 14: Cut the opening cords and push the loose ends inside.

Step 15:
Add a dab glue on the top and bottom of the opening to secure the knots. Dry overnight.

Step 16:
Push the bottom ends inside using a pencil or crochet hook. To hang, poke a strand of cord through the top and make a loop.

Tip: Make an oblong nest by adding more center rows above and below the opening.

CRAFT 11: SUNSHINE TREE OF LIFE

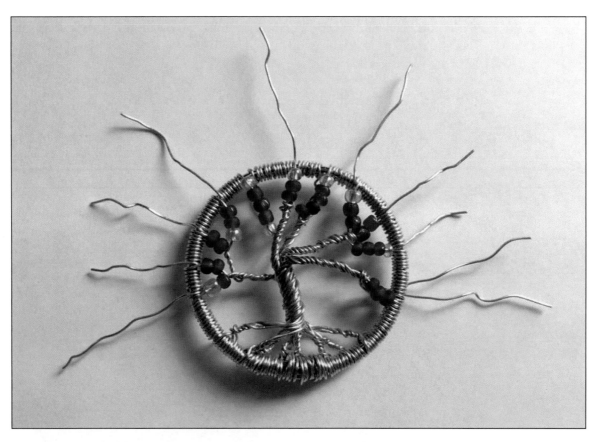

Design this beautiful decorative pendant that you can hang from a chain as an ornament or place inside a small shadow box like a prized heirloom.

Materials:
Steel wire
Book rings (2")
Assorted beads (small)

Tools:
Needle-nose pliers
Wire cutters, Ruler

Estimated Time: 3 hours

Level: Advanced

Cost: Just $.50 with leftover supplies to make five more!

Step 1:
Cut 9 lengths of steel wire 21" long.

Step 2:
Fold each wire in half, then wrap from the center of each wire both ends around the base of the ring two times each. Put one or two tightly on both sides of the bottom hump in the ring, then work toward the center. Use tape on the ring to keep them from slipping around. Be patient, this step is not easy.

Step 3:
Divide the 18 wires into consecutive groups of three, then twist them at the base with pliers to form the roots. Only twist about 1/4" for the center root groups, and about 1/2" for the outside roots.

Step 4:
Gather all wires into the center and tightly twist several times to form the trunk. Make sure you only go about to the middle of the ring to leave room for your branches.

Step 5:
Divide the 18 wires into three groups of 4 wires and two groups of 3 wires. Twist each of the groupings several times to form branches. Leave room to add beads at the end of each wire before they reach the ring edge.

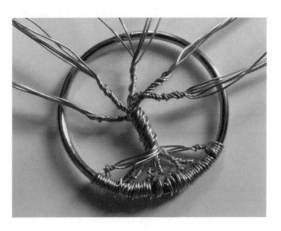

Step 6:
Add a couple of beads to each wire out to the edge, then wrap the end tightly down to the lower branch on the ring. This will fill out the space on the ring. You may have to cut 2-3 wires off early and twist up branch to hide.

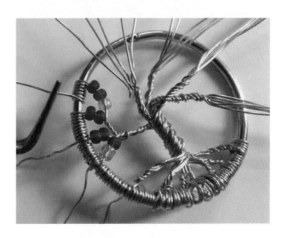

Step 7:
Cut the ends off in a sunshine pattern as shown in the final picture. You can also cut them to the ring and twist with pliers to the inside to prevent sharp edges. Hang from a chain as an ornament or pendant, or just display it.

CRAFT 12: SHADOW BOX FRAME

Create a nice shadow box from any picture frame. Use it to conceal your artwork, or create your own miniature scene. Everything looks special when it's behind glass.

Materials:
Picture frame (8" x 10" or less)
Poster board (white or color)
Black electrical or duct tape

Tools:
Scissors or X-acto knife
Pencil, Ruler, Clear tape

Estimated Time: 30 minutes

Level: Intermediate

Cost: $3 with leftover supplies.
One shadow box about $1.30!

Step 1:
Remove the glass from the picture frame and trace it onto a sheet of poster board

Step 2:
Measure the desired depth of your shadow box (1/2" to 1") and draw another box outside of the first box. (Half an inch shown below)

Step 3:
You should now have two boxes with lines extending all the way out.

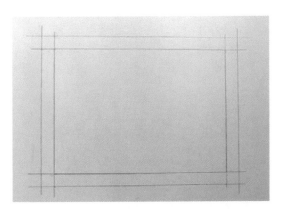

Step 4:
Using the back of the X-acto knife, or a thin flat-head screwdriver, score along the lines.

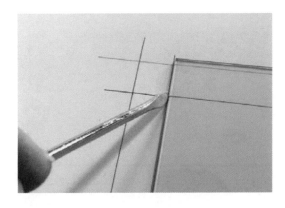

Step 5:
Cut along the outside rectangle.

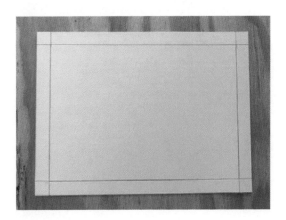

Step 6:
Make a cut from the outside to the inside box on the four top and bottom vertical lines.

Step 7:
Flip the sheet over and fold up the edges of the inside rectangle. The pencil marks will be on the outside.

Step 8:
Fold the corner flaps over the outside so they will not be visible on the inside of the box. Tape them up with clear tape. You may want to cut the tape width in half if too wide.

Step 9:
Design your shadow box interior (See Craft 13). You may want to cut another piece of poster board just slightly smaller than the glass to use as a backdrop, or to attach an item to. When done, glue it to the back of the box interior.

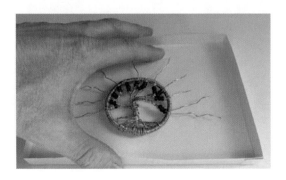

Step 10:
Place the glass back into the frame and use two thin strips of clear tape per edge (8 total) to hold it in place. Make sure they cannot be seen from the front of the frame.

Step 11:
Insert the completed shadow box into the back of the frame. It will fit rather snugly. Make sure the frame metal tabs (if any) are on the outside of the box. You may want to remove them with pliers beforehand.

Step 12:
Use the black tape to attach the box to the frame with the tape along sides and frame.

Step 13:
Tape the picture frame hanger board to the back of the box using the black tape. Make sure the hanger and standup arm are in the correct position.

Step 14:
When all tape is secure all the way around, display your new shadow box!

Important: When creating shadow boxes that will hang on the wall, make sure you don't put too much weight inside. You don't want anything breaking should the electrical tape loosen. You may want to use strips of stronger duct tape to hold the box to the frame, then cover it with black electrical tape—or use black duct tape.

More Ideas:
Use color poster board, tissue, or wrapping paper for interesting backgrounds.

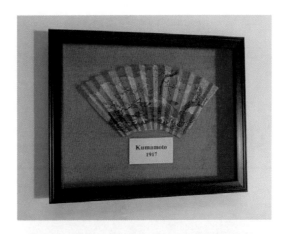

CRAFT 13: SHADOW BOX INTERIOR

Create shadow boxes for holidays. Or make a garden scene with packets of seeds and dried cuttings. Or how about a Dinosaur Jurassic Park? Let your imagination run wild!

Materials:
Picture frame (8" x 10" or less)
Poster board (white or color)
Black electrical or duct tape
Decorations for inside

Tools:
Scissors , Knife, Glue stick/gun
Pencil, Ruler, Double-stick tape

Estimated Time: 1-2 hours

Level: Intermediate

Cost: Depends on decorations.

Step 1:
Make your empty shadow box using the instructions in Craft 12. Do not tape it to the frame yet.

Step 2:
Measure a strip of foam to be about 1/4" less than the depth of the box.

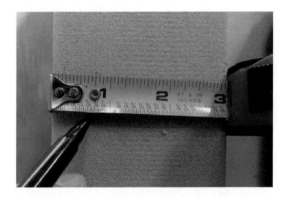

Step 3:
Use a miter saw or a knife to cut the strip.

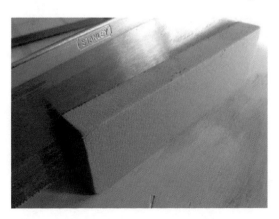

Step 4:
Here I cut an uneven curve to alter the height of my ground floor.

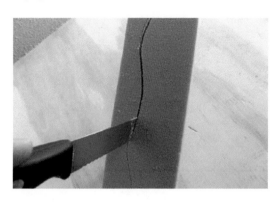

Step 5:
Place the pieces inside the box to see how it looks. I cut another piece to fit the box length.

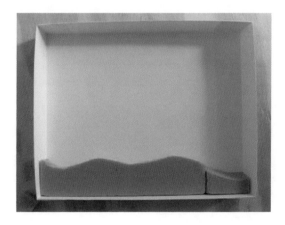

Step 6:
Prepare your interior decorations. Here I am cutting the wooden stems shorter on the eggs.

Step 7:
Position your decorations. Test looks.

Step 8:
I added a bunny cutout to add depth.

Step 9:
You'll want to try different backdrops as well. Printed photos, paper, burlap, etc.

Step 10:
Add a drop from glue gun to the wooden ends before placing them back into the foam.

Step 11:
Run a glue stick on the back of the box, making sure to cover the corners well.

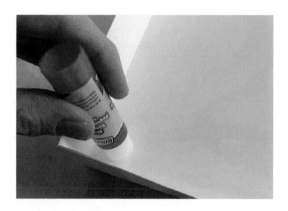

Step 12:
Attach your backing. I also added strips of a printout on the sides to give it a 3D effect. Place deep in the corner so no gaps show.

Step 13:
Use double-stick tape or a glue gun to adhere items. Glue gun works better with Styrofoam than floral foam for a more permanent hold.

Step 14:
I added decorative shred to conceal the floral foam. Make sure nothing extends too far above the top of the box so the glass can fit.

Step 15:
As in Craft 12, use clear tape to hold glass.

Step 16:
Tape box inside frame with electrical tape as in Craft 12. With a deeper shadow box, you may need to go around several times to hold it and cover the white of the box.

Step 17:
Tape the stand to the back as in Craft 12 and display!

Important: When creating shadow boxes that will hang on the wall, make sure you don't put too much weight inside. You don't want anything breaking should the electrical tape loosen. You may want to use strips of stronger duct tape to hold the box to the frame, then cover it with black electrical tape—or use black duct tape.

CRAFT 14: DECORATIVE STRING BALLS

You've seen them in catalogues. Now you can make decorative string balls with just balloons and glue. White glue is often sold at dollar stores around back-to-school time.

Materials
Jute or Cotton twine
Balloons
White Glue and Petroleum jelly

Tools
Scissors, disposable container,
Plastic or newspaper drop cloth

Estimated Time: 30 minutes

Level: Intermediate

Cost: About $.25 per ball.

Step 1:
Cut jute or cotton twine into 30-foot lengths for each ball. This gives adequate coverage.

Step 2:
Blow up balloons to the desired ball sizes. Tie ends securely.

Step 3:
Rub a thin coating of petroleum jelly over each balloon.

Step 4:
Pour a bit of white glue into a disposable container. Then soak the entire string.

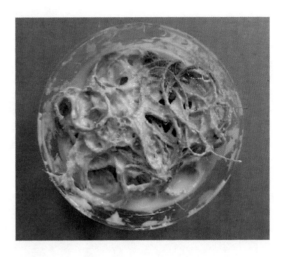

Step 5:
Run string through your fingers to remove excess glue.

Step 6:
Wrap the string around the balloon. Try to overlap and cover as much as you can. Allow to dry overnight. Pop and remove balloon.

CRAFT 15: PLASTIC BOTTLE FLOWERS

Why throw your plastic bottles away when you can create these beautiful flowers! Any size will do. This is a fun craft meant for adults since it involves working with a flame.

Materials:
Plastic bottles, Permanent markers, Silk flower stalk with nickel-sized round centers

Tools:
Scissors/snippers, Pliers, Drill, Tea light, Matches, Glue gun

Estimated Time: 1 hour/flower

Level: Advanced

Cost: $6 with vase and beads. Use markers many times over.

Step 1:
Cut the top and bottom off a plastic bottle as shown using sharp snippers or scissors. Snippers are better for thicker plastic bottles.

Step 2:
On the top portion, make even cuts from the base to the neck. Remove the date stamp with fingernail polish remover if possible.

Step 3:
Do the same with the bottom. You can make as many cuts as you want depending on how many petals you want.

Step 4:
Shape the tips of the petals with scissors or snippers. Look at flower patterns for ideas.

Step 5:
In a well-ventilated area, hold the flower with a pair of pliers and allow the petals to hover over a tea candle about an inch. Move away if they curl too quickly. You can always reheat and pull out a petal to straighten it out. Be careful of the hot flame!

Step 6:
Here are the top and bottom shaped as flowers. Take your time to add character.

Step 7:
Color the petals with permanent markers. These were done with the marker brands shown in the Materials pictures. Color both sides thoroughly. Allow to dry overnight.

Step 8:
For stems, separate the silk flower tips and discard (or reuse later) the silk flowers.

Step 9:
Drill a hole in the center of each cap large enough to fit yellow flower center stem.

Step 10:
Thread the caps over each bare stem, screw the caps back onto the flowers, then reattach the flower centers.

Step 11:
Put a dab of hot glue on the back of each cap and push and hold center to seat it in the cap.

Step 12:
Arrange in a vase with colored beads.

46

More Ideas:
Use more than one color on each flower.

Create stamens by cutting every other strip smaller and melting them to the center.

Or find silk flowers with removable stamens and pistils that you can insert into the caps.

Cut super-thin petals for wispy flowers.

Use nail polish for more opaque flowers. You will need to apply several coats.

Important Tip: Permanent markers tend to fade in bright sunlight, sometimes in a matter of days. If using markers, it's best to illuminate the finished flowers with artificial light or keep them indoors away from bright windows.

RECIPE 1: PARMESAN PEPPERONI PIZZA

Enjoy a scrumptious Parmesan cheese and pepperoni pizza in just fifteen minutes! The ingredients listed below are those readily available at Dollar Tree. Excellent pizza sauce!

Main Ingredients:
Camillo's Pizza Crusts (2-pack)
Hormel Pepperoni (2-pack)
Rinaldi Pizza Sauce
Grated Parmesan Cheese
Oregano Leaves

Staple Ingredients:
Butter

Estimated Time: 15 minutes

Level: Easy

Cost: Approx. $1.30 per pizza!

Ingredients purchased at Dollar Tree

Step 1:
Preheat the over to 450° F. While you are waiting, roll a stick of butter over the top and edges of the pizza crust.

Step 2:
Add three large spoonfuls of pizza sauce to coat the center of the crust.

Step 3:
Sprinkle on a nice coating of Parmesan cheese, then a thin layer of oregano leaves. Allow the Parmesan to coat the crust edge.

Step 4:
Add one packet of pepperoni.

Step 5:
Sprinkle on another thin layer of oregano.

Step 6:
Turn the oven down to 425° F and bake on the center rack for 7-10 minutes or until lightly brown. Remove from oven and cool for five minutes before eating. Bon Appétit!

RECIPE 2: POTATO ALFREDO BURRITOS
with BBQ sauce and Bacon!

Make these delicious potato burritos with a tangy and creamy Alfredo/BBQ sauce mix. I used Dollar Tree's Chef's Essence™ Alfredo and Kraft™ Spicy Honey BBQ sauces. Add bacon to the burritos for extra crunch! Makes a great meal or snack anytime.

Ingredients:
Medium Tortillas (10-pack)
Tater Rounds
Alfredo Sauce
Spicy Honey BBQ sauce
Turkey bacon (optional)

Estimated Time:
15-20 minutes

Level: Intermediate

Cost: About $.60 per burrito!

Step 1:
Mix two large spoons of Alfredo sauce with one spoon of BBQ sauce for each burrito. Place in the refrigerator to chill.

Step 2:
Cook about 8-10 tater rounds per burrito following the instructions on the package.

Step 3:
While the tater rounds are in the oven, cook one or two bacon slices per burrito following the instructions on the package. Here I chose to cook the bacon along with the taters. Just make sure your bacon is cooked thoroughly.

Step 4:
When the taters and bacon are done, place tortillas on top of the tater pan to warm up.

Step 5:
Lay down your bacon, add your tater rounds, then spoon on the Alfredo/BBQ sauce mix.

Step 6:
Roll the wraps, folding the bottom up after the first roll, and serve!

Tip: I discovered that the Tuscan Garden® Spicy Ranch dressing at Dollar Tree also makes a good sauce in place of the Alfredo/BBQ mix. Save a dollar!

RECIPE 3: ALL-PURPOSE BURRITO DIP
with Cheese, Beans, Beef, and Rice!

This all-purpose dip can be served with crackers, rolled into tortillas, or spread onto hamburger buns for a quick and delicious meal or snack. Items purchased at Dollar Tree.

Ingredients:
Old El Paso™ Cheesy Nacho Bowl
Southgate™ Chili with Beans
Crackers, Tortillas, or Buns

Estimated Time:
10 minutes

Level: Easy

Cost: $3 with crackers, tortillas, or hamburger buns. Serves 4-6.

Step 1:
Fill Cheesy Nacho Bowl with hot water to about 1/4" below the fill line. This will make the dip less watery. Place in microwave and follow heating instructions on the box.

Step 2:
While the Cheesy Nacho Bowl is cooking, warm the can of Chili with Beans on the stovetop. Stir occasionally.

Step 3:
Once cooked, stir the Cheesy Nacho Bowl to help dissipate the steam and allow the rice to soak up the water. Let it cool for a minute.

Step 4:
Fold the Cheesy Nacho Bowl into the Chili with Beans and stir. Leave a little to place on top of the finished serving bowl.

Step 5:
Pour into a serving bowl and add a dollop of sour cream if you like. Serve with crackers. Reheat the next day for a thicker dip!

Step 6:
You can also roll the dip into tortillas, or spread it onto hamburger buns for Cheesy Sloppy Joes! A little goes a long way.

RECIPE 4: PEACH FIZZ & PEACH SHAKE

Nothing tastes better after a long day than a refreshing peach fizz or peach shake. The shake uses Cookies and Cream ice cream for a unique flavor. The peach fizz drink is easy to make in large quantities for a friendly gathering. Two drinks for two occasions!

Ingredients:
Peach Fizz: Jumex Peach Nectar
Stars & Stripes Peach Fruit Mist

Peach Shake: Cookies and
Cream Ice Cream, Jumex Peach
Nectar, 2% Reduced Fat carton
Milk, frozen peaches (optional)

Estimated Time: 5 minutes

Level: Easy

Cost: (10) 10-ounce fizzes for
$2. About $1 per shake.

Peach Fizz:

Step 1:
Mix a 2/1 ratio of the Peach Fruit Mist to the Peach Nectar for a single drink.

Step 2:
Place a peach slice over the edge or within the drink itself. Serve with a straw.

Tip: If you want to make a batch for a party, just pour the two bottles into a punch bowl as is! The peach nectar is sold in a container half that of the Fruit Mist, so the ratio is correct.

Peach Shake:

Step 1:
In a blender, mix 1 cup Cookies and Cream ice cream (about 3 heaping spoonfuls) with 1 cup peach nectar and 1/2 cup milk. Add more milk if too sweet.

Step 2:
Pour into a wine glass and place a peach slice over the edge if you like. Serve with a straw.

Tip: Place a few frozen peaches into the mix to make it more of a smoothie shake.

RECIPE 5: CHOCOLATE KISS ACORNS

An easy chocolate treat that's perfect for the holidays or anytime. And it doesn't take that long to make. Just piece together, chill, and pop them out when your guests are ready!

Ingredients:
Vanilla wafers (Bite Size)
Hershey's Kisses® (18 per bag)
Semi-sweet baking morsels
Chocolate frosting

Estimated Time:
10 minutes

Level: Easy

Cost: About $1.30 for 18 acorns. Plenty of leftover frosting, vanilla wafers, and morsels.

Step 1:
Chill the Hershey's Kisses® and semi-sweet baking morsels for at least an hour before working with them. This way they won't melt in your hands!

Step 2:
Dab a bit of chocolate frosting onto the base of the large Kisses. Adhere to the flat part of the Vanilla wafers.

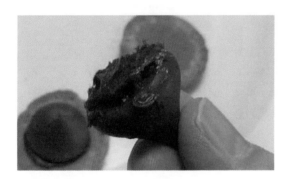

Step 3:
Dab a tiny bit of chocolate frosting onto the base of the baking morsels. Adhere to the top center of the Vanilla wafers.

Step 4:
Gently place finished acorns into a plastic container. As soon as possible, place the container into the refrigerator so the frosting hardens up a bit.

Step 5:
Just before serving, place the finished acorns onto a serving plate. If you want, set some fake autumn leaves under the plate and make it a centerpiece.

Step 6:
Enjoy with a tall glass of milk!

ABOUT THE AUTHOR

I hope you've enjoyed working on these crafts and trying out some of the recipes. It was my pleasure putting this book together. I am also the author of several novels and the producer of several films. You may have seen my *Beyond the Garden Gate* nature film—a year in the life of a garden set to soothing music—on PBS. All of my DVDs and books are available on **Amazon.com** and **victorrook.com**. Happy crafting and happy reading!

People Who Need To Die

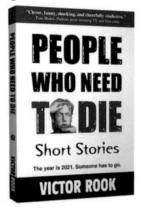

A fed-up society in the year 2021 chooses to eliminate bad drivers, obnoxious cell phone users, mean neighbors, litterbugs, spammers, and more. Funny, satirical horror.

In Search of Good Times

A troubled man goes on a road trip to find the fictional sitcom families from *Good Times* and *All in the Family*. Nostalgic, though set in 2009.

Musings of a Dysfunctional Life

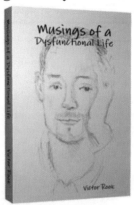

Humorous and poignant anecdotes about life, religion, sex, ghosts, aging, music, and more. Something everyone can relate to when they approach middle age. My memoir.

Beyond the Garden Gate

A year in the life of a garden set to music. Winner of two Telly awards with music by Emmy-nominated composer Matt Ender.

Calmness of Woods

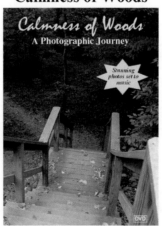

A photographic and musical journey through the beauty of woodlands. Includes a tutorial on how to take better pictures.

Victor J. Rook